Time to

by Paula LaRosa

Dale and Jane want a ride.

It is time to tug.

Pile on top, kids!

Take a fine ride!

The van can not go.

It is time to tug.

Mike can put on a wire.

Mike can fix the tire.

Look at the kite dive!

Tug on the line, Jane!

The kite can rise.

The kite is fine.

It is time to tug.

See what can tug.